FUNKOFIED:
TRANSFORM YOURSELF INTO A FUNKO POP! CHARACTER WITH AI MAGIC

A Step-by-Step Guide to Designing Your Custom Funko Pop Avatar using AI Technology

Steve K. Bryant

Copyright

CONTENTS

INTRODUCTION

A summary of the customizability and popularity of Funko Pop! Figurines

As collector icons, Funko Pop! Figurines have made a name for themselves by portraying a variety of pop culture, TV series, movies, and video game characters. These vinyl figures have captured the attention of collectors all around the world with their characteristic oversized heads, expressive eyes, and small bodies. Funko Pops are unique in that they feature a wide range of characters, from musicians to superheroes, which appeals to a specific market of collectors and enthusiasts.

B. Overview of the Microsoft Designer prompt for utilizing AI to create customized Funko Pop! figures

Microsoft Designer is an AI-powered creative application that has recently garnered attention for its unique feature that lets users create custom Funko Pop! avatars. Through a series of questions, this program uses artificial intelligence (AI) algorithms to translate word descriptions into graphic representations. This allows users to create Funko Pop! figurines that are either themselves or fictional characters.

C. The article's goal is to show readers how to use AI to make a Funko Pop! of themselves.

This post provides a thorough tutorial on how to use the prompt function in Microsoft Designer to create a Funko Pop! figure that is a perfect replica of the author. It seeks to encourage readers to embrace the trend of customized Funko Pop! avatars and employ AI technology creatively by guiding them step-by-step through the process.

D. A succinct description of the procedure and its current social media fame

Users' curiosity and excitement have been aroused by the current spike in popularity surrounding the development of personalized Funko Pop! avatars on social networking platforms. Sharing their own Funko Pop! figures online has become popular, thanks to the Microsoft Designer prompt's accessibility and ease of use. This phenomena has gained popularity quickly, inspiring others to investigate this recently discovered medium for artistic expression.

The method of turning verbal cues into visually beautiful representations is unique and easy to understand, which makes it appealing to a broad audience.

Using AI to create a personalized Funko Pop! means more than just creating a digital representation—it means giving your name or your favorite characters a distinctive, collectible form. The appeal is in being able to create something truly original within the context of this widespread collection trend.

This new trend represents the nexus of pop culture, technology, and creativity and ushers in a new era when people may effortlessly transfer their imaginations into tangible digital forms. This post aims to explain the process via the lens of AI so that readers can participate in this creative movement and create their own Funko Pop! avatars.

CHAPTER 1:

Funko Pop! and Personalized Avatars

Funko Pop! has carved a niche in the world of collectibles by capturing the essence of beloved characters and celebrities in adorable, stylized figurines. These vinyl figures, characterized by their oversized heads and small bodies, encompass a wide array of pop culture icons, spanning movies, TV shows, comic books, and more. What sets Funko Pop! apart is its ability to encapsulate the essence of characters, making them instantly recognizable despite their minimalist design.

The allure of Funko Pop! lies in its expansive range, which appeals to diverse fandoms. From iconic superheroes like Batman and Spider-Man to beloved characters from franchises like Harry Potter, Star Wars, and Game of Thrones, Funko Pop! figures offer something for every enthusiast. The collectible nature of these figurines has led to a fervent community of collectors who seek out rare editions, limited releases, and exclusive variants to add to their collections.

B. Limitations of the Official Funko Pop! Design System.

While Funko Pop! has garnered immense popularity for its extensive lineup, the official design system for creating custom figurines on their website is somewhat limited. This platform restricts users to a predefined set of choices, offering a finite selection of clothing, accessories, and companion options. Consequently, the customization options are constrained, limiting the extent to which users can personalize their figures to match their unique traits, styles, or preferences.

Moreover, the official Funko Pop! design system often lacks the granularity required to accurately represent specific individual features or distinctive clothing choices. This limitation detracts from the personalization aspect, resulting in figurines that may not capture the nuances and details desired by individuals aiming to create a faithful representation of themselves or others.

C. Introduction to Microsoft Designer's AI-based Prompt for More Personalized Creations.

To overcome the limitations of Funko's official design system, users have turned to Microsoft Designer, an AI-powered design tool that introduces a new avenue for crafting personalized Funko Pop! avatars. Leveraging the capabilities of OpenAI'sDall-E 3 text-to-image AI generator, Microsoft Designer empowers users to generate highly customized figurines by inputting specific prompts.

The introduction of Microsoft Designer's AI-based prompt system marks a significant advancement in creating personalized Funko Pop! avatars. Unlike the constrained options provided by Funko's platform, this AI-driven tool allows for greater creativity and specificity. Users can input detailed descriptions of desired features, attire, accessories, and even packaging, enabling a more accurate representation of themselves or envisioned characters.

Microsoft Designer's prompt system harnesses the capabilities of AI to interpret textual prompts and generate corresponding visual representations. By providing detailed descriptions, users can fine-tune their prompts to match individual attributes, ensuring a closer resemblance to their physical appearance, style, and personality. This level of customization surpasses the constraints imposed by the official Funko Pop! design system, offering a more tailored and personalized experience for enthusiasts and collectors.

In essence, Microsoft Designer's AI-based prompt system revolutionizes the creation of Funko Pop! avatars, providing a platform where users can exercise greater control and creativity in designing figurines that closely mirror their desired traits and characteristics.

CHAPTER 2:

Using Microsoft Designer for Custom Funko Pop

The world of Funko Pop! figures has expanded beyond popular characters to personalized avatars, thanks to Microsoft Designer and its AI capabilities. Crafting your unique Funko Pop! representation involves a few steps within this user-friendly tool. Let's delve into a detailed walkthrough to help you create your custom Funko Pop! avatar.

A. Accessing and Utilizing Microsoft Designer

Getting Started:

Access Microsoft Designer through your web browser.

If you don't have an account, sign up or log in to your Microsoft account.

Navigate to the AI prompt feature within the Designer tool.

Understanding Microsoft Designer Interface:

Familiarize yourself with the layout and options available for inputting prompts.

Explore the functionality and tools provided for generating AI-driven designs.

B. Sample Prompt and Breakdown

Constructing a Sample Prompt:

Consider specifying features like gender, ethnicity, clothing, and accessories.

For example, "Create a Funko Pop! avatar of a male wearing a blue superhero costume with a red cape and mask, holding a shield."

Breaking Down the Prompt:

Explain the significance of each detail in the prompt and how it contributes to the avatar's creation.

Highlight the role of specific prompts in shaping the avatar's appearance and characteristics.

C. Tips for Creating an Accurate Avatar

Specifying Details:

Emphasize the importance of providing detailed prompts that reflect personal features accurately.

Include elements like hair color, facial expressions, attire, and any distinctive accessories.

Adjusting Prompts for Accuracy:

Guide users on refining prompts by tweaking or adding specific details to improve likeness.

Advise on experimenting with different combinations of prompts for varied results.

D. Discussing Result Variation and Prompt Refinement

Understanding Result Variance:

Explain the possibility of receiving multiple avatar variations from a single prompt.

Highlight how slight changes in prompts can yield significantly different results.

Refining Prompts via Editing:

Discuss the option to edit prompts post-generation to enhance accuracy.

Share insights on using the editing feature to refine specific avatar details.

Creating your personalized Funko Pop! avatar via Microsoft Designer involves providing detailed prompts, understanding result variations, and utilizing the edit function for accuracy. This process empowers users to craft unique representations that closely resemble their desired likeness.

CHAPTER 3:

Legal and Precautionary Considerations for Custom Funko Pop! The avatars

While the creation of customized Funko Pop! avatars with Microsoft Designer's AI prompt inspires creativity, there are a number of safety measures and legal ramifications related to this cutting-edge trend that need to be taken into account. The combination of artificial intelligence (AI) and user-generated material frequently results in the need for rules and limitations, particularly with regard to names, copyright, brand representation, and compliance.

Microsoft's Guidelines for Responsible AI and Limitations on Real Names.

The prompt-based AI system in Microsoft Designer demonstrates responsible AI principles meant to protect user privacy and uphold moral standards. Interestingly, there are limitations on using real names in the prompts on the platform. This limitation is consistent with Microsoft's dedication to protecting user privacy and identity. When creating Funko Pop! avatars, users are urged to use unique variations or pseudonyms in place of real names.

By using genuine names with caution, we hope to ensure that personal information is not misused and that privacy laws are followed. Users can enjoy the creative process of creating customized avatars without sacrificing their privacy or going against Microsoft policy by using pseudonyms.

Talk about Possible Copyright Disputes Between Funko and Microsoft.

The relationship between the AI prompt system in Microsoft Designer and the production of Funko Pop! avatars brings up relevant questions about possible copyright violations. Funko, a company well-known for its collectible figurines of celebrities and other characters, might be protected by copyright laws for its unique brand aspects, such as logos, designs, and the aesthetic features of its Funko Pop! figures.

Microsoft's contribution to the development of avatars that resemble Funko Pop! figures may result in complicated legal issues concerning intellectual property rights. Although consumers use the AI prompt to design these avatars, Microsoft may come under fire for being linked to Funko's exclusive trademarks and images.

Distinguishing the Avatars from the Official Funko Branding.

Although the creation of Funko Pop! avatars with Microsoft Designer's AI has generated a lot of excitement, it's important to recognize that these user-generated avatars are not the official Funko branding. The avatars created by the prompt display differences and alterations from the original Funko Pop! figures.

These variations could be in how Funko's unique logo is used, changes made to the typography, or an incomplete depiction of trademark features connected to Funko's branding. Even though some avatars could resemble some parts of Funko's designs, they frequently don't have the exact details or brand names that are essential to the actual Funko Pop! merchandise.

Conjecture on Microsoft's Potential Defenses against Copyright Violations.

Should Microsoft and Funko engage in copyright issues about the use of AI prompts to create Funko Pop! avatars, Microsoft's defense would likely rely on adhering to copyright regulations and implementing appropriate AI practices.

Microsoft can argue that their AI prompt system is just an artistic tool that lets users create customized avatars using prompts they supply. The business may stress that the generated avatars are user-generated content and that Microsoft has no control over the particular information or components that users select from within the prompts.

Furthermore, Microsoft may contend that the avatars' accidental departures from legitimate Funko branding components came from the AI's interpretation of user cues rather than a purposeful effort to mimic Funko's copyrighted content.

In the end, Microsoft might want to handle any possible legal issues around the production of Funko Pop! avatars while showcasing its dedication to user privacy protection, ethical AI usage, and copyright compliance.

In conclusion, it's important to take into account the safety measures and legal issues mentioned above, even if creating customized Funko Pop! avatars with Microsoft Designer's AI prompt offers a creative and fascinating new way for self-expression. Respecting copyright rules, following responsible AI principles, and being aware of how official branding differs from other branding are all crucial when working on such creative projects.

CHAPTER 4:

Social and Ethical Consequences of the Funko Pop! Avatar Movement

The usage of Microsoft Designer's AI prompts to create customized Funko Pop! avatars has become more popular, and this trend has received significant attention on social media. People creating Funko Pop! figurine replicas of themselves or famous people is a craze that has generated a lot of ethical and social discussion, illuminating its origins, effects, and possible consequences.

Acknowledgment of Source and Pervasive Application.

It's still unclear where this trend originated. It appeared out of nowhere, almost over the course of a weekend, and quickly captivated users, who jumped at the chance to create their own Funko Pop! avatars. The fad quickly gathered hold and spread like wildfire throughout multiple social media sites, even though there was no obvious instigator. Particularly on Twitter, there was a surge in shares as people showcased their own Funko renditions, encouraging a feeling of communal involvement.

Prioritizing Pleasure while Handling Potential Problems.

Participants in the trend can certainly find entertainment and inspiration from it, but it's important to proceed cautiously and be aware of any possible problems. The company Funko Pop! is well-known for its collectible figures, many of which feature celebrities or licensed characters. Making customized avatars could violate intellectual property rights and cause Microsoft and Funko to dispute copyright.

While enjoying the trend's fun and creative aspects, participants should be aware that there may be legal ramifications. Microsoft's AI prompt may unintentionally violate Funko's proprietary designs even while it encourages creative expression. Users that follow this trend should therefore proceed with caution and moral responsibility.

Recognizing Origin Uncertainty.

The fact that this trend started on its own creates a cloud of doubt about who started it. Its lack of a single, easily recognizable creator feeds rumors regarding its origins. It's unknown if the trend was initiated by a community or influencer, or if it was the result of a single person experimenting casually with the Microsoft Designer prompt. Although intriguing, this ambiguity also begs concerns about the trend's viability and possible consequences.

Warning AboutFunko's Response.

Given Funko's exclusive nature and brand identification, it is possible that the corporation will respond to the growing popularity of this fad. The licensed characters and distinctive designs of Funko Pop! figurines make them stand out as collectors. If Funko feels that these customized avatars violate their intellectual property, it may take legal action or take other steps to preserve the integrity of its brand.

Participants and onlookers should be aware of Funko's possible response and realize that the company's position may have an impact on the trend's continuation. This careful approach emphasizes how important it is to respect intellectual property rights, acknowledge the limits of artistic freedom in the digital sphere, and strike a balance between ethical issues and creative expression.

Finally, the rise and quick spread of customized Funko Pop! avatars offer an intriguing fusion of artistic expression and possible moral quandaries. The trend encourages fun and participation in online communities, but it also brings up issues with brand integrity, intellectual property, and the appropriate use of information created by artificial intelligence. In the digital age, ethical concerns and artistic expression must coexist peacefully only if ethical standards are followed, the trend is enjoyed responsibly, and potential repercussions are considered.

CHAPTER 5:

Public Participation and Exchange

Social media is full of interesting trends these days. One such trend that has sparked a creative and enthusiastic frenzy is the prompt-sharing practice of creating customized Funko Pop! avatars. People have been joyfully sharing their experiences and the adorable results of using the Microsoft Designer prompt to create Funko Pop! replicas of themselves on a variety of social media channels, including Twitter, Instagram, and more.

What started out as a simple prompt-based exercise has quickly grown into a popular fad that encourages people to be creative and have fun. The idea is straightforward yet incredibly captivating: users enter particular information about themselves into the Microsoft Designer prompt to create a customized Funko Pop! figure that reflects their physical characteristics, style preferences, and even imagined personas.

This trend's appeal is derived from its ease of use and the delightful surprises it offers. Users can create fanciful and artistic versions of themselves as Funko Pop! toys, or they can produce uncannily realistic depictions of themselves as they experiment with different prompts. This trend has quickly acquired traction, capturing the interest and involvement of a wide range of people, from casual social media users to pop culture aficionados and tech experts.

Motivation for Involvement and Trials.

This trend's inclusiveness and the freedom it provides for personal expression are what make it so beautiful. It's a broad invitation to everyone to explore their creative side, regardless of their background in art or design. People can use the Microsoft Designer prompt as a blank canvas to let their creativity run wild and customize it to represent themselves as Funko Pop! characters that best capture their individuality and sense of flair.

For those who are thinking about following this trend, it's a very simple and fun approach. Through adjusting the prompt's parameters—such as the attire, haircuts, accessories, or even the color schemes of the Funko Pop! box—participants can watch as the AI generates endearing depictions that frequently provide happiness and surprise.

An Invitation to Participate and Exchange.

While creating these Funko Pop! avatars is exciting and fun, sharing is what really propels the trend forward. Not only is it fun to create these charming representations, but it also spreads a sense of community and camaraderie by sharing the results with a larger audience.

This post invites all readers and social media users to actively participate in this movement in order to further strengthen the sense of shared enthusiasm. Take advantage of the Microsoft Designer prompt's creative path, create your own unique Funko Pop! avatar, and then share it with the world in an exciting way.

People can display their creative Funko Pop! avatars in the comments part of this article, on forums, on social media, or on other sites. Talk about the joy these creations have brought you, the experiences you had, the prompts you utilized, and the unexpected peculiarities in the generated avatars.

Final Thoughts.

The popularity of creating personalized Funko Pop through prompt sharing! Avatars are a celebration of uniqueness, creativity, and the joy of sharing—they are more than just digital representations. It serves as a reminder that self-expression and whimsy have a place in our everyday lives.

So, to all of you readers and fans out there, take advantage of this chance to become lost in the realm of original artwork and customized avatars. Play around with the prompts, let your creativity run wild, and then show off your Funko Pop! creations to the community online. Let's work together to turn this trend into evidence of the boundless creativity and good humor that connect us on social media.

CHAPTER 6:

Conclusion

summary of the article's key ideas and the reasons why making Funko Pop! avatars is appealing.

We've explored the fascinating world of customized Funko Pop! avatars made with AI (more precisely, Microsoft Designer's prompt engine) in this post. The focus has mostly been on the shortcomings of the official Funko Pop! design method and the substitute path provided by Microsoft's AI-powered tool. By entering certain characteristics, users can create highly customized Funko Pop! figurines that closely resemble them in terms of appearance and style.

This page explains the procedure, gives readers advice on how to use Microsoft Designer efficiently, shares tips for creating precise prompts, and gives instances of well-known characters made using pseudonyms. It has also drawn attention to the ingenuity and enjoyment that go into creating these avatars, as well as any potential difficulties users may run into, like limitations on using real names and any copyright issues.

Concluding remarks regarding the trend's present status and possible durability

Currently, the practice of creating customized Funko Pop! avatars with Microsoft Designer is gaining popularity on social media and drawing fans from a wide range of platforms. The level of participation and excitement displayed by this trend at the moment demonstrates the general public's interest in personalized figurines that capture unique characteristics and trends.

The duration of this tendency is still unknown, though. Even though it has gained a lot of traction, a number of things may affect its sustainability. The durability may be impacted by Funko's reaction to this creative use of AI, by any copyright-related legal ramifications, or even by shifting consumer preferences for internet trends. However, it appears that making customized Funko Pop! avatars is appealing to a wide range of people, suggesting that this trend may continue in the near future.

A friendly reminder to enjoy the trend while exercising caution on any possible copyright issues.

While designing one's Funko Pop! avatar can be exciting, it's important to keep copyright issues in mind. Although it allows for creative expression, Microsoft's Designer prompt operates in a gray area of the law, particularly when it comes to the unlawful use of Funko's logo and product imagery. This serves as a warning to users, asking them to respect the trend and be mindful of any possible legal repercussions when using copyrighted content.

A final request to readers to create and share their Funko Pop! avatars in order to join the trend

This post invites any readers who are curious about the idea of creating their own Funko Pop! avatar to explore the trend. Try playing around with the prompt engine in Microsoft Designer to embrace the creativity and excitement. Create a customized challenge by adding your distinct characteristics, fashion sense, and maybe even a dash of whimsy. Explore the possibilities of AI-generated personalized art by sharing your works, participating in the discussion, and becoming fully immersed in this captivating trend.

The article urges users to enjoy the enjoyment of creating these avatars while respecting intellectual property rights and being aware of the consequences of their actions. It also calls for responsible and courteous involvement.

Not only is it a creative and fun exercise, but employing AI to create Funko Pop! avatars is a reflection of the increasing fusion of technology and artistic expression. The article's main points are summarized in this conclusion, which highlights the necessity of engaging responsibly with this emerging trend while also stressing its enjoyment.